Volume V Number 1

Yale Anglers' Journal

An Undergraduate Publication

New Haven

Editor-in-Chief	David Haltom
Assistant Editor-in-Chief	Molly Worthen
Business Director	Alexis Peter Surovov
Art & Marketing Director	Andrew Liverman

Editorial Board: Colin Bennett, Kate Block, Mike Doran, David Haltom, Chris Heaney, Mike Kai, Laura Koo, Andrew Liverman, Jamal Miles, Brook Sprague, Alexis Surovov, AJ Weissler, Molly Worthen
Copy Editor: Sarah Post

Advisor at Large & Co-Founder:	Joseph Furia
Advisor at Large & Co-Founder:	James Prosek
Advisor at Large:	Steve Hayhurst
Faculty Advisor:	Nelson Donegan

Mail: Yale Station, PO Box 204048, New Haven, CT 06520-4048
Phone: (203) 432-0268. Fax: (203) 432-0357. E-Mail: info@yaleanglersjournal.com
Fishing the Web: http://www.yaleanglersjournal.com

The *Yale Anglers' Journal* (ISBN 1-892441-08-X) is a registered non-profit undergraduate publication dedicated to an understanding of angling and the natural world, with an emphasis on estuaries, streams, rivers, lakes and oceans. This journal is published by Yale College students; Yale University is not responsible for its contents.

Guidelines for Submissions: Prose, poetry, art, and letters to the editors should be sent on computer disk or via e-mail in cut-and-paste text form, or, if this is not possible, by mail. **Please include a short biographical sketch**. The Journal will respond within 60 days, but will not comment or offer suggestions. Honoraria are currently not available. Submissions not accepted for a current issue may be included in a later one. Submissions will be returned upon request. Views and opinions expressed in articles in the Journal do not necessarily reflect the views and opinions of the editorial staff.

For Subscription: The Yale Anglers' Journal is published semiannually. Single copies $12, available by mail, www.yaleanglersjournal.com, or at selected bookstores. One year subscription $20; two year subscription $30. Gift cards with personalized messages can be included when subscribing a friend. Donations to the *Journal* are accepted in the form of checks made payable to Anglers' Journal.

Front Cover - *Guide and Salmon,* Oil on Canvas by Galen Mercer, © 1997.
Back Cover - *Untitled Painting,* Japanes Watercolor on Paper Artist Unknown

Printed by Reprographics and Imaging Services, Yale University
© 2001, Yale Anglers' Journal, Inc.

Roster of Patrons

Editor's Note

When I arrived at Yale in the fall of 2000, I hesitated to jump right into extracurricular activities, deciding to first see how much time academics would demand, and settling into life at school. Around Christmas I had decided to try to find an organization that I could join that would be interesting, fun, and different. I had recently become interested in flyfishing—recently because I grew up in Mississippi, and fishing with flies is rare to say the least—so I set out to find a group that would at least let me go out fishing occasionally.

I knew I had seen something about a fishing organization on campus at some point, but I could not remember where or when. In scouring lists of undergraduate organizations, the only group I could find that bore any resemblance to an actual fishing club was some literary publication called the *Yale Anglers' Journal*. I really did not know what I was getting myself into when I wrote an email to "Alexis or Whomever It May Concern" on the Journal staff, saying hesitantly that I "would very much appreciate the opportunity to speak with someone on the staff

… about any prospects for participation in the Journal that may be available."

I expected some rigorous application process involving writing samples and interviews, and instead I was invited down to the office, where I was told promptly that I was on the staff. Well, that was easy enough. Within the next month, I had spent a weekend ice fishing at James Prosek's house in rural Connecticut. Now I'm the Editor-in-Chief. What's not to like?

There has certainly been work involved, and the future is especially bright for the *Journal* right now because we have been able to build on several successes we have had in the recent past. Our website, *www.yaleanglersjournal.com*, has allowed us to easily reach a broader market, as the huge increase in subscriptions over the past year indicates. Since this past summer, we have added some two hundred new subscribers. Here at Yale, a *Journal*-sponsored Swedish Fish-eating contest in November successfully gained us much notoriety on campus; we hope to institutionalize the contest as an annual event.

Additionally, our presence at two flyfishing tradeshows in 2001 and especially our trip to Denver this semester have given us the opportunity to spread the gospel of the *Yale Anglers' Journal* to a much wider audience. The *Journal* has made many friends at these shows, and we have received countless new subscriptions and submissions from folks we met.

While we finished the '00-'01 school year with five staff members, more or less, (depending on whom you ask), this year we are very excited about a great new group of Yanglers—some seniors, a couple of juniors and sophomores, and several freshmen—who have helped us immensely in the publication of this issue. Several new opportunities have recently arisen to expand the range and scope of the *Journal*'s business, and we are eagerly pursuing them. With another issue due out this spring and our annual dinner scheduled for April 18th, we have much more work, and much reward, to look forward to.

I hope you enjoy this edition of the *Yale Anglers' Journal*, as we have all worked hard to publish only the highest quality literature and art. We believe that many of the submissions we received and published in Volume 5 Number 1 are second to none.

Sincerely,

David B. Haltom
Editor-In-Chief

Advisor at Large

Heading into my senior year I feel like a held-over brown trout surrounded by a new group of finglerlings hand-selected and stocked by the University's admissions office. My time at Yale has been well spent. In between schoolwork and editing and working on the *Journal*, I have spent some (never enough) of my free time on the water fishing (notice I did not say catching) as well as a great deal of time running as a varsity athlete on the Yale Cross Country and Track teams. I have enjoyed leadership positions as editor of the *Journal* and captain of my team.

I started out as a small fish in a big pool, and after four years I have grown to be larger, although not fatter due to my rigorous training schedule. While I'll never grow to be too big a fish for this institution, I am now ready to move onto larger pools, like Manhattan, with new fish.

After a successful day on the upper Housatonic River, on one of my many runs, I became aware of the numerous parallels between my two recreations. Running, like angling, provides me with time and isolation for reflection. For me both fishing and running are enjoyable and peaceful endeavors that allow me to connect with nature. They have their own languages, special equipment, friendships, and peculiar traditions, which sometimes correspond in the most unlikely ways—as evident by my favorite track event, the steeplechase, where goldfish are traditionally released into the water pit. (I hope to raise the bar of competition by bringing a fat rainbow trout to a track meet one day.)

Between my two passions I have discovered a fascinating relationship; while running, I am the animate object floating through the air over the ground, and when fishing I am the stationary fixture in the middle of a flowing and ever-changing stream.

Tight Lines as Always,

Alexis P Surovov

Alexis Peter Surovov
Advisor at Large
Editor-in-Chief '99-'01

Yale Anglers' Journal

Volume Five   Number One

Essays and Poetry

The Companion	Abu Faruk	15
It Has Orange Teeth	Sydney Lea	23
Confessions of a Reformed Purist	Hartt Wixom	27
Re-Lax-Ness	Jim Murphy	35
Rummaging Through the Basement Finding Piscatorial Audubons	Robert Behnke	37
James Prosek on Izaak Walton	James Prosek and Steve Sloan	45
Winter Kill and other poems	Thomas Barnes	55
Hunting the Hunt	James Rudaitis	61
Theodore Gordon	Austin McK. Francis	75
Why Men Fish	Scott Starbuck	83

The Angler's Study

An Angler's Commentary on the Salvage Logging Rider	Richard K. Stoll	89

Hook, Line, and Sinker

Closing Day	James Rossbach	93

The Seine Fishnet
From the Tomb of Rahotep, Medum
Dynasty IV

The Companion
Abu Faruk

W hat I will always remember is the heat. Heat is the one thing you can never escape. Twenty-four hours a day you are uncomfortable—even at night the heat overrides everything. It is impossible to sleep, but if the evening winds roll over the river, you have a reprieve from the discomfort and the mosquitoes, so you pray for the winds. But here is the Nile, one of the greatest rivers in the world, and suffering is part of the adventure. The roots of civilization sprang from the Nile waters, and its allure brought me here.

I looked upon this trip from Alexandria to Aswan as a cleansing. I had just ended a long-term relationship—or rather, she ended it—and I had just finished a grueling prelim examination for my doctorate. Grueling only because I had gone through the system rapidly, and they wanted me to pay. I paid.

The early morning smells on the Nile are unique: an acrid burnt odor hovers over the land, evidence of the countless dung-fueled fire hearths in the pleasant homes and along the river. Once you have experienced it, you'll never forget that smell. If you are lucky, there is a faint mist, the shabura; you cannot see it, but you can feel it. The disturbing part of the experience is that the more comfort the mist brings you, the hotter the day will be. The locals warned me of this, and they were right.

I had been working on the river for over two weeks, collecting the Nile's fish and examining their diversity. Two months prior, I was in the Western Desert directing an archeological project; the predominance of fish remains at this remote site prompted me to search for a specialist to analyze the recovered bones. Because there was no authority to call upon, at least none that had been alive in the past fifty years, the task fell on me. If I were to finish my dissertation, then I had to identify the fish bones. To identify the fish, I needed modern examples for comparative analysis. It was a challenge I willingly accepted.

Having grown up on the waters of the Puget Sound, fishing the lakes and streams of Idaho and Washington all my life, I felt at home on the river. Sitting on a boat in the water felt natural to me, although outfitting provisions for the trip was a little different. Back home we adhered to the fisherman's basic food groups: caffeine, sugar, alcohol and salty snacks. Here, alcohol and salty snacks took a back seat to caffeine with plenty of sugar. My fishing partners Ibrahim and Hashem took caffeine consumption to its highest limits, knocking back shot after shot of syrupy tea by the hour. A tall cool one would certainly have made the fishing easier!

We were in search of the *Isher Bayad*, better known in English as the Nile perch, the largest freshwater fish in the world. These fish easily reach six feet in length and can weigh over two hundred pounds. I had a modest research stipend, but by Egyptian standards, I was rich, and thus we were well outfitted with bait and tackle. I took my trusty salmon rod with me, which the locals referred to as "the club." It was a stout rod, with a deep-sea salt-water reel. Nothing fancy, but it had brought in its share of salmon and halibut off the coast of Washington.

Yet, with all the gear, the best of bait, and amiable, knowledgeable fishing companions, we had no fish. By the third day, my two compatriots began to mumble the name "Faruk." My Arabic was good enough to understand most conversations, but they knew that if they spoke rapidly and whispered, they could get complicated scenarios by me. What I did pick up was that Faruk was some sort of guru or mystic, and in his company things happened—fish were caught and in great quantities. Finally, after a fifth day of heat and no fish, Ibrahim approached me about Faruk. If we wanted the *Isher Bayad*, we had to try to bring Faruk on board. My first impression was that this was a scam and how much was it going to cost me to bring another of their buddies on board for a free fishing trip. I countered their request with a monetary limit for supply costs for an additional person. Both Ibrahim and Hisham looked puzzled. Finally, Hisham stepped in and with great reverence said that Faruk would come aboard of his own free will: he could not be coaxed, and he could not be intimidated or bribed. Faruk had no need of money. He chose to go and to do what he wanted and with whom he wanted. If we were lucky and if Faruk approved of us and came aboard, we would certainly be blessed with fish.

My interest was piqued, and seeing that, they explained further. Faruk was a mystical figure to the local fishermen. Egyptian fishermen, like all fishermen, are very superstitious. As we moved to an area of the river where Faruk was known to make occasional appearances, they introduced me to some of the Faruk fishing lore. In the area we were to soon fish, he could appear—any time, anywhere. His presence always was an omen for good fishing. Ibrahim said there was a time when three men were pulling in a two-meter long Nile Perch. They had worked it all day and finally were able to bring it along side their small craft. After lashing it to the gunnels, they headed back to shore for a rest. There, somehow, sitting in the forward seat was Faruk. Hisham, not to be outdone, told of a time when late at night they had gone into a military zone to fish, thinking it would be rife with big ones. The area had not been fished in ages because of the army presence. Quietly and secretively, they positioned their small boat in the middle of the river and waited for a strike. Although risking a jail sentence or worse, they stuck it out and caught a beautiful string of bolti, many exceeding twenty-five pounds. As they came to shore, they saw movement in the bulrushes that lined the bank; they feared the worst, then out popped Faruk. How he got into a military area under total light surveillance, electronic surveillance, cameras, and a dense minefield, no one knew.

As an anthropologist, I knew that from a purely cultural perspective, I had to meet Faruk. For a day an a half I waited.

On the morning of our seventh day of fishing for the

perch, Faruk walked on board. Faruk swaggered around the boat as if he owned it; he was arrogant with the attitude of a gangster. He was important, a boss, and he knew it. He looked us up and down; my companions held their breath, for this was a meeting with local fishing lore, with Nile royalty. I was totally shocked by his presence and watched him closely. He was nothing like I expected. He was a connoisseur of disgusting, scratching at his privates as nonchalantly as if he were scratching his head. He turned his nose up at fresh fish or meat and dined happily on a salvaged road kill he had intended to use for bait. Mouthwash not being big in these parts, I hoped our meeting would not include the customary cheek kisses. I even witnessed him urinate on the leg of a local tradesman we had lured in hopes of acquiring some gas for our stove—it was little surprise to me that no gas was forthcoming. In short, I did not view him as a savior but a social liability, and I can honestly say that concerns for the quality of prose prevent discussing the "full milieu" of his habits.

Although I tried to keep my distance, particularly after the gas salesman affair, Faruk latched onto me. Ibrahim and Hisham were overwhelmed with joy that we were deemed acceptable company. I believe they were equally as happy that they were not singled out for special attention as I was. In fact, Faruk kept in such proximity to me that they began referring to me by the honorable title Abu-Faruk.

We began fishing in earnest with a newfound confidence. Sure enough, within hours "the club" began to dance, and my reel began to sing. I had hooked a big one. While I worked feverishly playing the fish, Faruk walking back and forth barking out orders: tip up, tighten the drag. After several hours, a six-foot Nile perch lay alongside the boat. It was true—Faruk had the power. As a reward he was given the cheeks of the fish, which he gobbled up eagerly. Faruk and I spent the next six months together, fishing. I managed to collect enough specimens to ensure completion of my dissertation as well as create a research collection unmatched in the United States.

When the time came for me to leave Egypt, I sat on the boat where I had shared so many adventures with Faruk, saddened by our imminent parting. Faruk, never much for conversation, stared at me with his all-knowing eyes as I contemplated this. We sat for probably an hour. I couldn't leave without him. I rushed to the embassy, finding sheer panic everywhere. I asked a Marine guard what was going on and found there was a crisis in Lebanon, and there was fear it might spread to Egypt. I told him I was trying to get out myself, but needed paperwork done for my companion. He allowed me in a side door and the appropriate paperwork was expeditiously completed and filed.

Next morning at the airport, Faruk and I found that our flight was canceled, the plane having never left New York. We could, however, hop a plane to—where else—Beirut, with a connection to Athens, then Rome, and finally the United States. We decided to take it and thirty-six hours later arrived in the United States. There were many incidents on the plane, including Faruk's independent attempts to gain special access to the mystery chicken dish served on board the flight, as well as an uncanny attempt to visit the city of Beirut under siege.

Faruk and I spent the next seven years together fishing. He was the best companion I ever had. And he *was* a mystic. Whenever he was on board, fishing was always spectacular. He had an innate sense of timing and territory, always knowing when and where to signal me to begin fishing. One would think that traveling to a new county, he would have been intimidated or even shy; this was never the case. I took him fishing everywhere. He was always sure of foot, even in roughest of waters. I never had to worry about him. He never wandered too far from the boat in unfamiliar areas or too close to unfamiliar people who might be prejudiced against his background. His complex nature clearly came through on our long fishing trips far from home. And, when I moved to Illinois to take a position at the university, he followed me. He was, as the Nile fishermen say, the "efreet"—the spirit, the one with knowledge.

What was most amazing about Faruk was that he was a cat, and I didn't even like cats. He was one of kind, more like a dog in his loyalty and ability to travel and nearly human in his ability to communicate. He was the greatest fishing partner I ever had and my closest friend. Faruk finally succumbed to a congenital defect in one of his circulatory valves, but sometimes, I can still feel his presence and can still hear him barking out orders from the bow of the boat.

Douglas Brewer (Abu-Faruk) is a Professor of Anthropology at the University of Illinois and Director of the Spurlock Museum of Culture and Natural History. He has written five books and published numerous articles on the archaeology and fauna of Ancient Egypt. Most of his early academic works focused on the fishes of the Nile and their archaeological remains. Although his present academic position is far from home, he still manages to fish the waters of Washington State for salmon and trout.

Bahamut
Marina Korenfeld
From the Encylopedia of Imaginary Beings
Watercolor

It Has Orange Teeth

After a story told me by the late Lesley Childs

Sydney Lea

He made it a habit to cast his <u>dorothea</u>
  —each night, all that June long—to one trophy trout,
whose skepticism cured Lesley of being a dreamer
for the moment; that was what fishing a fly was about,

he told me: the world come down to pure concentration.
You saw the rise, you threw a line above it,
no further thought entered—not self, not family, not nation. You
were both away and clearheaded. That's why he loved it,

remotely like loving your way through a tumble of water,
mindful only of boulders and eddies, the rest,
the universe, having shrunk. There was only disaster
if he let his mind or canoe go anywhere else.

He said that he timed false casts to his quick breath's rhythm,
then dropped the dun on the slick, while overhead bats
and swallows were hunting, although he didn't see them.
(Everything superficial, I punned.)
                      The slap

behind him felt something, therefore, akin to the blow
a sheriff once fetched him. The cop suspected narcosis,
not his first <u>grand mal.</u> What oddly had seemed like a flow
in his life—a current bound to draw him the closest

he'd ever get to a kind of blessed distraction—
turned into a mangle of strobe-light, obscenity, threat.
That night it was only a beaver, whose own concentration
lay in getting her way to the west, to her twig-hungry kits.

Bank-beavers, he said, whose home "weren't no more than a hole
in the high-rolling tier by the rapids," which Lesley at last
was compelled to notice. Cliché came to serve him: "My soul,"
he said, "was all nightmares: present, future and past,

"and each ran into the other, and each of them nameless."
The beaver's a creature so placid you might call her staid.
In fable, she represents the virtue of habits,
but her warning caused Lesley to hear rebukes from the dead

for spending his time in trying to obliterate time;
he'd spent too much at conniving to get himself laid,
or at trout or at poker, nights when he should have been home,
too much in indifference, his wife lying cancerous in bed.

Les reeled, then stuck his fly in the rod-grip's cork.
The beaver pounded again, then glided cross-river.
Dizzy, he feared a siezure there in the dark
for the first time in years. Had he taken the pills? He shivered.

After that evening, he never again went out wading.
It seemed hard enough to get through a day on dry land.
He never made out what the river-ghosts had been saying.
Yet they had addressed him, he knew. And a terror remained.

Sydney Lea (Yale BA '64, Saybrook. Ph.D. '72, Comp. Lit.) is author of seven collections of poems, most recently Pursuit of a Wound *(September '01). He has also published the flyrishing novel,* A Place in Mind, *and a collection of angling and hunting essays,* Hunting the Whole Way Home. *Recipient of fellowships from the Guggenheim, Rockefeller and Fulbright Foundations, Lea founded and for thirteen years edited the* New England Review. *He is currently a teacher of writing at Dartmouth College.*

A PROPOS DU CLUB DES PECHEURS A LA LIGNE

—Ça mord, quelle chance !
—Je vous défends d'attraper un poisson avant moi; n'oubliez
pas que je suis votre Vice-President.

Honore Daumier
Cartoon
1842

Confessions of a Reformed Purist
(Or, Getting Along with Fishing Snobs)
Hartt Wixom

In the beginning, I tried to uphold the highest and noblest of angling ethics.

It came naturally to me. Put me behind a car wheel and I'd yield at intersections to vehicles three-quarters of a mile away. If I saw a sign on a city street which said, "No Spitting," I didn't dare clear my throat. I once wrote a letter of apology to the FBI for tearing off the inspection tag from my mattress before getting it home.

It stood to reason then that when I took up the noble sport of fishing I adhered to its loftiest standards. I was inspired by the Roman, Martial, and the astute Greek, Aelian, and of course the English aristocrat, G. E. M. Skues, all of whom agreed a trout should be enticed only by the feathered replica of an insect and that on the surface via barbless hook. Following proper protocol to its zenith, I further concluded that a fish ought to be honestly hooked in the upper jaw to be considered fairly caught. Anything less would be demeaning to both victor and vanquished. Hatchery fish must not, of course—unless vaccinated and pedigreed according to the rules of the Catskill Fly Fishers Club—be confused with those born free. And all fish, however caught, must be immediately granted an honorable release.

Later, I read and concurred most emphatically with Theodore Gordon, that patron saint of American fly fishing, that not only should an artificial fly ride high but only the lower extremity of hackles could be allowed to dip beneath the surface. Since there were no good dry fly fioatants on the market, I experimented with various kitchen concoctions. One part glue to four parts vinegar proved smelly, yet prevented the fly in the sink from submerging to a shameful low. In actual current, the artificial had to be "doctored" often to keep it at a regal high. In heavy flow, I found I had to douse the fly every other cast. But, of course, it had to be done.

In rigidly adhering to The Purist's Code (TPC), I felt myself singularly buoyed above the common morass of anglers; those un-name-able riffraff who cast bait with splash poles and recline in easy chairs all day—while no doubt perusing pornographic literature.

Looking back on it, such strict adherence to TPC did of truth somewhat delay the catching of my first trout; yet in following the rules I reasoned that one must not lower the bar to allow compromise. Lower one's standards but once, i.e. fish with contraband such as weighted nymphs, and one might also in time succumb to lures, natural baits, cheese, corn, and the most tempting of the garbage swills: garlic marshmallows.

In an effort to catch my first trout from a small creek near my home, I studied the clear water profusely. Ten casts with a royal coachman, dry, drew nothing but contempt from the nearest target tinning beneath a copse of brush. Twenty casts later, the fish utterly refused to rise to that point where water met sky. In fact, every time I cast to the surface, the fish fled to the bottom.

Given time—several more months—I observed trout finning near my fly. Were they becoming curious about my artificial? No, merely amused by it; I watched them, cotton-white mouths opening and closing like clockwork, tails up, nose down, degraded to groveling for insects in the stream gravel. Bottom feeders. I could not sink to such a low. All of angling-dom's hallowed saints were watching. I turned from this sultry siren song—departing empty, it is true—but with head held erect. Nothing could seduce me into this or any other corrupt act of icthyological depravity. I would uphold the honor of Martial, Aerial, Skues, Gordon.

Some temptations were, of course, egregious. Noticing my lack of success, a cousin slid over to me and said, "Here, try some of these." He handed me a mix of salmon egg clusters with Velveeta. He molded it together into a sort of jelly, smashed it tightly onto a hook, tossed out, and immediately caught a 12-inch rainbow. I chastised him most roundly for this, but he only shrugged and caught another fish on the next cast. If without scruples whatsoever, one might also use dynamite— or simply dry up the stream.

Most of that summer passed without my locating any trout that would abide by TPC. In late August I vacated my nondescript gray hackles to a size 16 Adams, female, spent, upright, dry (of course), after ceremoniously anointing it with my special dry float formula. I caught nothing with it, but I did feel the ghost of Mr. Skues hovering over my shoulder, at times whispering encouragement. With these wispers came a certain tinge of smugness that placed me above the heathen caste of common but misguided anglers.

Then came the day I cast the Adams deftly to a surface-feeding trout. It finned precariously close to my offering, snapped its jaws once in my direction, then swam to the bottom of the pool and ate a worm protruding from the mud.

I went home and dreamt of the brown trout that had almost pulsated my rod tip. The warm glow of this experience sustained me for the next week. On the following, I studied Walton: "Make your placement under the sun so as to not cast a frightening shadow." I also created an artificial hatch by casting my female Adams, dry, a hundred times to one pool as pre-scribed by Dame Juliana Berner (that patron saint of all women everywhere, who was possibly the first fly fisher; why N.O.W. has not made more of her is a mystery for Sherlock Holmes). Alas, I caught nothing but a cold, standing in the rain casting to trout which probed wickedly among rocks along the stream bottom.

What if I was with a crew of Theodore Gordon Fly Fishers from upstate New York who went down in a plane, along with their fly fishing accoutrements, over the East Fork of the Delaware? Would they all starve to death before anyone condescended to try a weighted nymph?

It was time to take drastic measures. I would vacate my home fishing haunts and make a pilgrimage to the shrine of all serious anglers: Montana's Madison River. There, at the Holy Grail of western American angling, a shrine even Theodore Gordon had not visited, in water that separated the top echelon of the pecking order from all Untouchables (bait anglers), surely I could catch a proper trout.

I even rented a raft. Putting in at the Varney Bridge, which seemed the proper thing to do during the salmon fly hatch of early July, I rounded my first bend. There on the bank before me stood a distinguished angler, as attested by his English hand-crafted Fedora, chest waders with the Montana Trout Unlimited Casting Club patch, gold-leafed grip-plated custom-made split bamboo rod from Argentina's Patagonia Fly Shop, Hardy reel, polarized glasses from Abercrombie and Fitch, with a monogram signature from both Homer Circle and Roderick Haig-Brown.

One could see even by the supercilious arch of his eyebrows—as I shot out of control into the sacrosanct riffle where he had just cast—that he was among angling's most noble, although at the moment angry, fishermen. He was to angling what a Stradivarius violinist might be to a depleted junior high school orchestra.

The raft apparently drifted too close, as evidenced by his clenched fist. "Clod!" he yelled at me. But it wasn't the raft that upset him so; apparently it was the rigging. My artificial floated close enough that he could see it was a huge salmon fly pattern, as I'd been advised to use by the man at the tackle shop in Ennis. "Adams, size 16, female, dry!" he shouted at me as my raft (picked up by the swift current) slammed into the tail of the hole. The gap now widened between us.

Not only the physical but the philosophical. I had sinned. The angler on the bank of the Madison River clearly represented the Grand Elite of all fishermen, and I had offended him. What to do? I decided my only recourse was to do penance by sitting down in my motel room and repeating over and over, "I shall not use cheese even during a cheese hatch and

I shall not use salmon flies during an Adams hatch, or at least when they should be."

The next day I felt better and went fishing again. This time I found myself on O'dell Creek, and once again a huge gulf separated me from the elite. Said the man across the stream, "Took a big rainbow this morning in the Watercress Pool." I saw that he was fishing the sector, as noted by the signs, that was closed to the public. "Cost me $250 a day per rod to cast over here but it was well worth it. Took the fish on a size 26 cowdung; had to wait until the emergence was over of course, to take him as an adult insect on top."

He didn't wait for an answer. "Best fish I've seen since England's Chalk Streams, the Itchen, you know...I..." By now I had moved out of earshot.

And then something snapped. Using phonies, were they? Well, I would use the real thing. Stooping to look beneath a rock, I found and impaled the real thing on my hook: a larval *Plecoptera* that would later hatch into a salmon fly. And it happened. I didn't want to make too much of my first trout, since I'd caught it with something the quarry could actually taste. I decided it would be best to forget about this seven-inch rainbow—pale, flaccid, fin-chewed—to never discuss the matter with anyone, and to remain nonchalant; but strictly for the record, it happened at Mile 17.6 on the Madison River at exactly 8:38 p.m. on July 16, a Friday with a glowing sunset, on 6-lb. test Rio leader and Scientific Angler weight forward No 6 line.

It felt good.

In fact, it felt so good that I decided to return to O'Dell Creek to see if I could repeat my accomplishment on a second water. I was about to turn over a stone to find uh, bait, when my friend of the day before happened by. He had a proposition. Would I be interested in joining the O'Dell Creek (Upper Crust) Anglers Club (OCUCAC)? It so happened they were short on funds this month and were offering for only $2,999.99 a year a membership providing angling rights on the 1.5 mile private angling side of the stream on Tuesdays and Thursdays between 9 AM and 1 :30 PM.

There were three requirements in addition to the

money: a new member had to (1) pledge within the coming year to visit Roscoe, N. Y., and spend one day on the Beaverkill, registration to be completed at Livingston Manor Town Hall, (2) hook and land one brown trout of four pounds or more on a size 20 or smaller midge, on any water of choice within the next six months, (3) give a report on how Grayling, Michigan got its name. Oh, and one more thing: I was not allowed to stomp on the bank to attract planted fish that had been raised in a hatchery and knew that it was feeding time by the heavy manner in which the hatchery man approached the water with a bucket full of meat pellets.

It all seemed simple enough. I could even mortgage my house to raise the initiation fee. But there was something about it that made me hesitate. It was the caste system. It was never reduced to writing, but it was plainly there. I felt no better nor worse than my peers. We were all just equals, were we not? Alas, no; for I saw at the invitation dinner (for prospective members) that he who had cast the smallest (dry) fly on the lightest leader to catch a trout, any size, was allowed to eat before the others were allowed to sit. The trouble was that when Percival Teitlebaum hooked his 8-inch brook trout on a "horsehair tippet" (of one-half pound, it was said), it took him 37 minutes to land the fish. Those in his way as he roamed up and down the stream were asked politely to give way to a certified Master Angler.

"Why," I asked, "go after a grizzly bear with a BB gun?" My question was not answered. In actuality I might say it was, to a degree, scorned.

After driving past the metal fly fisherman statue casting on the western edge of Ennis, I went to the General Store, bought a dozen nightcrawlers, and returned to the Madison. On the first cast, I hooked and landed a beautiful 16-inch brown. Then another on the next cast.

"What did you entice him on?" called an excited fisherman across the river.

"Garden hackle," I replied. "Size 6. Wet. I keep them alive in peat moss."

Since then, I have continued to deteriorate until Skues

and the others would scarcely recognize me. But as Thoreau once said, "Everyone should believe in something. I believe I'll go fishing." I'm sure he used worms, too, else why would he want to continue fishing in his old age?

I have refused, however, to succumb to angling with swill offerings such as power bait. I do, after all, have some scruples remaining.

Yet, the other day the same cousin who offered me salmon eggs mixed with cheese...that cousin...well, he showed me a most resplendent brown taken on green power bait. It got me started thinking...

Hartt Wixom, 67, has spent a lifetime hunting and fishing (and writing about it) across the western United States, Alaska, Mexico, and Canada. He was Rocky Mountain field editor for Field and Stream *magazine, Wyoming editor for* Western Outdoors, *and a frequent contributor to* Outdoor Life, *in addition to writing with many other magazine stories and countless newspaper columns. While an outdoor writer for the* Salt Lake City Deseret News, *he won two national awards for "telling it like it is" outdoor feature series. He also has several outdoor books to his credit, including* Elk and Elk Hunting, Fishing and Hunting Guide to Utah, *and* Improve the World -- Go Fishing. *Wixom retired from teaching college journalism at Brigham Young University in 1998. He and his wife Judene have seven children and shuttle residences between Cokeville, WY and Ivins, UT. At the present, Wixom is an outdoor columnist for the St. George, Utah* Spectrum.

The Fisherman
Jean Louis Forain
Oil on Canvas

Re-Lax-Ness

Jim Murphy

The floating stones once held by the fire
Drift down now to the sea.
Working up the river,
Lax makes memory from strong desire,
As I make mine of me.

A land, its blinds half drawn
Sleeps against the mist grey night.
The villagers lay face up,
Content to store the soft long light.

The glacier melts in the summer sun
I'm lying in the grass undone.
The land is moving, not the river,
Fire's now the steam it does deliver.

Jim Murphy is a man of letters and former owner of numerous college book-stores. Now best known as the founder and owner of the Redington Flyrod Company, he is an infamous and well liked member of the flyfishing community and currently lives in Stuart, Florida, with his wife and four children.

Great Lakes Steelhead X
Alberto Rey
Oils on Plaster

Rummaging Through the Basement Finding Piscatorial Audubons

Robert Behnke

T wenty five years ago the College of Veterinary Medicine vacated a WPA era building on campus and it was turned over to our expanding Department of Fishery and Wildlife Biology. At the time, I was in need of space for my collection of trout specimens and for a great volume of books, journals, literature, notes and files I had accumulated over many years. I was allotted a large area of the basement where I unloaded my goods and set up shop.

Over the years the Fishery and Wildlife Department continued to grow and more space for faculty and graduate students was needed. The old basement would be torn out and reconstructed. All of my possessions would have to be removed. A worst nightmare became a reality.

A large part of my time in recent months has been devoted to sorting through boxes, shelves and file cabinets to decide what to save and what to dispose of—separating wheat from chaff. Sorting through the files turns up some interesting bits of historical miscellany.

A newspaper clipping from 1974 reported that the first Atlantic salmon had returned to the Connecticut River. The story included a prediction that 30,000 salmon would be returning to the Connecticut River in 30 years (still have three years to go). With this clipping was a copy of a special supplement to the Greenfield, Massachusetts Recorder of June 8, 1990. A new

$17 million anadromous fish research laboratory on the Connecticut River at Turners Falls, Massachusetts was to be dedicated. The new research lab would be operated by the U.S. Fish and Wildlife Service with an annual budget of $1.7 million. The main emphasis of research would be Atlantic salmon, especially the restoration of salmon to the Connecticut River. A sophisticated computer model predicted that by the year 2021, returns of Atlantic salmon to the Connecticut River would reach 38,000. This reminded me of what I have written about the "illusion of technique" where sophisticated but simplistic models are often a poor substitute for knowledge and a deeper understanding of the subject matter.

The greatest number of Atlantic salmon counted in the Connecticut River since the first one was recorded in 1974 was 529 in 1981 followed by 70 in 1982 and 39 in 1983. Since then, despite great increases in hatchery production and stocking, salmon returns to the Connecticut River have run between lOO and 300 in most years.

A file drawer contained correspondence, notes and photos covering many years of communicating with some dedicated people, who like myself developed a passion, almost an obsession, to find and learn about rare and vanishing forms of trout.

I first met Bob Smith in 1975. At that time Bob was a recently retired waterfowl biologist with the U.S. Fish and Wildlife Service. He was an avid angler who had attained a stage of angling satisfaction whereby his greatest pleasure was derived from catching and photographing all of the species, subspecies, and distinct races of North American trout. This passion for wild native trout culminated in Bob's book: *Native Trout of North America* (Frank Amato Publications, Portland, OR: first edition 1983, second, revised edition 1994). Bob Smith did an excellent job of interpreting my publications on trout evolution, until then largely confined to the scientific literature, and making them available to the angling public. He became an effective crusader for the preservation of wild, native trout.

Bob Smith's book encouraged others to develop similar interest in native trout. Kyle McNeilly of Calgary, Alberta made contact with both Bob Smith and me to further his interests in putting together a museum-quality exhibit of realistic taxidermy models of all the forms of trout covered in Bob Smith's book. In return, Kyle helped Bob Smith to find and catch the "Sunapee golden trout" from an Idaho lake. The "golden trout" of Sunapee Lake, New Hampshire was an Arctic char left over from the last glacial retreat. It has been long extinct in Sunapee Lake, but some eggs had been shipped to Idaho in the 1920s and stocked into a few cold mountain lakes (see Sunapee golden trout in spring 1984 *Trout*). Bob Smith was elated to learn he now had an opportunity to catch a true Sunapee trout to add to his life list of rare trout and include in the second edition of his book. By the time Bob had arranged his Idaho trip in search of the Sunapee trout, Kyle McNeilly had already been there and filmed the Sunapee trout. Later, Kyle made a return trip, coming down from Canada to meet Bob at the Idaho lake where Smith caught, photographed and released the Sunapee trout to fulfill his dream.

I had the opportunity to see Kyle McNeilly's exhibition of trout replicas at a trout conference in Alberta in 1999. It is an amazing one-of-a-kind exhibit. Truly a labor of love.

Glen McFaul of Arizona is another angler with a deep fascination for rare, native trout. Glen carries a portable aquarium to photograph live fish. Glen has traveled much of the western U.S. checking on sites where I found rare trout from 25-40 years ago. His photographs and observations on the current status of many rare trout have been a help to me in keeping up-to-date on extinction threats. Page 142 of my 1992 monograph on western trout mentions that the known natural distribution of the rare Colorado River subspecies of cutthroat trout was extended to the Escalante River drainage based on Glen's finding a population there in 1991.

Perhaps the most unusual of these modern day trout Audubons is Johannes Shoffmann of Austria. Although Johannes is not an angler, he lives out his obsession for rare trout in his far-flung travels from China to North Africa. He dons a wet suit and enters the fish's domain. He makes observations and captures specimens for further study with a net.

In the winter 1986 issue of *Trout* I wrote about brown trout, I mentioned a relative of the brown trout that I named as a new species, *Salmoplatycephalus*. The new species was known only from three specimens collected from a river in Turkey in 1966. I also discussed a peculiar trout described in 1924 as *Salmo pallaryi* from Lake Algueman, Morocco. I made a request for anyone who might have any information on the status of *S. platycephalus* or *S. pallaryi* to please let me know.

Johannes went to Turkey and sent me photographs and detailed notes on *platycephalus* that he found in a spring-stream. Its distribution is restricted to a small area of the river drainage and its continued existence is threatened by sediment loading from agriculture and road-building. Johannes went to Morocco and verified that *pallaryi* is extinct, but found that the diversity of the native brown trout of North Africa has its origins in at least two separate invasions of two distinct ancestors (Johannes preserved tissue samples from the trout he collected for use in molecular genetic research).

Johannes also made surveys and collections to determine the status of some peculiar trouts of Adriatic drainages: the marble trout, *S. marmoratus* and the "soft mouth" trout of the genus *Salmothymus*. He found that both are now very rare; their original distributions have been greatly reduced.

After returning home from his expeditions, Johannes writes up a report of his findings including detailed taxonomic descriptions, life history observations and an analysis of the threats to continued existence of the rare forms of trout. He publishes the reports in an Austrian fisheries journal. When I read Johannes' scientific papers, the range and depth of knowledge displayed indictates formal training in ichthyology. When I later learned that Johannes is a baker by profession and a pure amateur ichthyologist, I was all the more impressed by his level of expertise. Johannes exemplifies the true meaning of amateur: one whose interest and enthusiasm for a subject is driven by love of the subject, not because it is part of their profession.

In 1995 I received a letter from a Yale student, James Prosek. James was then putting together a text to go with his paintings of trout in what was to become a highly popular book: *Trout, an Illustrated History* published by Alfred Knopf in 1996.

James inquired about trout in the Tigres-Euphrates basin (did a trout stream run through the Garden of Eden?). Johannes Shoffmann had recently sent me a paper on his expedition to record the characteristics of trout native to the Tigres drainage of Turkey (this was the first description of Tigres trout in the world literature).

James Prosek was planning a trip to Europe and I suggested he contact Johannes Shoffmann. With two such passionate trout lovers getting together, wonderful adventures were bound to be forthcoming. In the first two trips, James and Johannes sampled the historical trout waters of Slovenia, Serbia, Bosnia, Croatia, Greece and Turkey. James wrote the story of their adventures including his portraits of the diverse forms of trout they encountered and published it, most appropriately, in *Audubon* magazine (Jan.-Feb. 1999).

In the summer 1992 issue of *Trout*, I wrote about grayling. I mentioned a specimen of a grayling-like fish in the fish collection of the British Museum. This specimen was brought back to England in 1897 by St. George Littledale. The specimen was considered so distinct that a new genus and species was described for it. The collection locality is stated to be: "South slopes Altai Mountains on Chinese territory" (Mongolia). This species has not been found since and there is no other record of a salillonid fish in south slope Altai drainage's in China (drainages toward the Gobi Desert). The mystery of the south slope Altai grayling set the stage for the next wonderful adventure of Johannes and James in search of the mystery fish. James and Johannes met in Ulan Bator, Mongolia, rented a Russian jeep and began their quest. I received a postcard from Mongolia relating that the jeep had four flat tires in the Gobi Desert. They failed to find the south slope grayling but encountered a known species of Mongolian grayling, *Thymallus brevirostris*, in north slope Altai drainages, part of a large internal basin. No other salillonid fish exists in the internal basin and the Mongolian grayling evolved as a predator on the several species of minnows it lives with. It attains the largest size of any species of grayling but is so little known that there is no official world record for Mongolian grayling. The most up-to-date account of the Mongolian grayling can be found in a paper authored by Johannes in the Austrian fisheries journal.

Last summer, James and Johannes traveled to Kyrgyzstan to find the easternmost natural distribution of brown trout—*Salmo trutta oxianus* of the Aral sea basin.

The small fraternity of piscatorial Audubons are composed of a disparate group whose common interest is their passion for learning about trout that goes well beyond the ordinary. How many potential new members might there be? Anyone out there interested in taking another look at the south side of the Altai Mountains?

Dr. Robert Behnke, a retired Colorado State University fisheries professor, is widely recognized as one of the world's leading experts on salmon and trout. Dr. Behnke has authored the book Native Trout of Western North America *as well as a series on native trout for* Trout *magazine. As the director of the World Salmonid Research Institute, Dr. Behnke has done extensive research into the fields of systematics, zoogeography, genetics, biology of endangered, threatened, and rare fishes, and he holds a Ph.D. in Zoology from the University of California, 1964.*

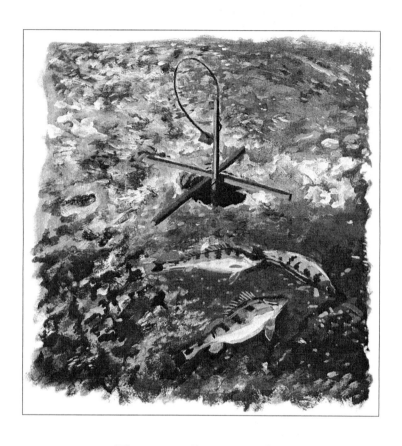

Tip-up on Bantam Lake
James Prosek
From *Joe and Me*
Watercolor on Paper
1997

James Prosek on Izaak Walton

An interview with James Prosek on Izaak Walton; Christianity and fishing; Milton, Donne, Cromwell and Eliot; and something called "technocracy"

James Prosek and Stephen Sloan

James Prosek is a graduate of Yale University with a degree in English Literature. He is the author, most recently, of *The Complete Angler: A Connecticut Yankee Follows in the Footsteps of Walton* (1999, HarperCollins, New York). Prosek began to fish when he was nine years old. Fishing provided solace, and eventually became a kind of religion, leading him on the trip that culminated in *The Complete Angler.* Written about Izaak Walton and his book by the same name (alternate spelling), Prosek's book is 322 pages of life philosophy and concludes, like the original, that everything the author does, whether it is fishing or not, is fishing. As Izaak Walton wrote in 1653, "*The Compleat Angler* is not about fishing, but about life. Or rather, it is about fishing--but fishing is life."

Prosek sat down to talk with Steve Sloan of "The Fishing Zone" radio show to discuss the larger issues behind the book.

Mr. Sloan: James Prosek has just written a new book that is a real treat; it's called *The Complete Angler: A Connecticut Yankee Follows in the Footsteps of Walton.* Tell us how this project got started. You were at Yale University when you decided to trace Izaak Walton's footsteps, so to speak.

Mr. Prosek: Yes. With my great interest in fishing influencing everything I do, I decided to write my senior thesis as an English Literature major on Izaak Walton and his book, *The Compleat Angler.* But really, this book isn't so much about what I wrote for my thesis; it's more about my travels through England and the people I met in Walton's wake.

Mr. Sloan: One astounding fact that jumps right out at the beginning is that *The Compleat Angler* is the most popular sporting book ever.

Mr. Prosek: It's actually the third most frequently-printed book in the English language, after the Bible and the works of Shakespeare.

Mr. Sloan: Yours is a book not only about fishing but also historical detective work, too, because you--and I don't know if it's ever been proposed before by anyone else--think that the words "compleat angler" were basically a pun, a disguised code for the times in which Walton lived, with Cromwell in his glory and raging through England, putting down Anglicans at every turn.

Mr. Prosek: Walton's book title was, as far as I'm concerned, code for "the Complete Anglican." Walton was a staunch Royalist ans a supporter of King Charles I when the Anglicans were being bashed by the Puritans. This was during the English Civil War in the 1660s, and Walton published *The Compleat Angler* shortly after the King had gotten his head cut off. Walton was certainly reevaluating his religious beliefs. It's not really a book of religious allegory or a polemic; it's a book on fishing. But some of his thoughts on the times generously leaked into his writing, I think. And it's also a book about how to live life simply and contentedly as a good Christian, a good Anglican. Walton quotes the Bible frequently and early on argues that all fishermen, like the apostles of Jesus, are good and follow peace.

We also know that Walton was a friend of John Donne,

and he also might have known John Milton, I'd like to believe, at the same time. Milton's *Paradise Lost* was published, I think, in 1667. *The Compleat Angler* had come out in 1653. It's interesting that they were published in the same churchyard, that they had the same publisher. So, it's possible that he and Milton could have come across each other. As I said, he likely knew John Donne well, and maybe even fished with him. When John Donne died, Walton wrote Donne's biography as a preface to the publication of Donne's sermons and poems. None of Donne's work was published while he was still alive. So Walton's first published work was his biography of John Donne.

Mr. Sloan: Tell us about the places Walton fished.

Mr. Prosek: Walton mostly fished chalk streams, which are a lot like certain limestone streams in Central Pennsylvania fed by big springs, usually with very clear, clean water. And a lot of the streams Walton fished are very much like they are today, but in part that's because they've been owned by the same families for centuries- members of the aristocracy. The water's mostly private, so the streams are in very, very good condition. Walton was born in Stafford in the Peak district, where there are many beautiful spring-fed streams, among them the Dove and the Wye. He lived his middle years in London and fished the Lea, a tributary of the Thames, which is where *The Compleat Angler* is staged. The last thirty years of his life he spent in Hampshire, in the south, where there are world-famous trout streams that come from limestone outcroppings and are very fertile because they have a lot of dissolved limestone that promotes insect life and plant life and makes for big, fat, healthy trout.

Mr. Sloan: When you fished them, did you experience a sense of history?

Mr. Prosek: Yes. It's possible that some of the fish were actually descendants of ones that Walton had caught. Sure, I was looking around for Walton's ghost. I met a lot of anglers who in some sense followed Walton; they were a kind of good, simple, content people-true servants and true disciples of Walton who enjoyed nature and fishing.

Mr. Sloan: You mention in the book that angling is joy but the minutia involved with it is really overdone today. For instance, I see fellows trying to fish with dry flies in high, discolored waters in March or April, proclaiming that that is the pure and only correct way of fishing. They know that they're not going to catch anything, but they actually disdain anyone who uses a wooly bugger or a nymph. I don't agree with this kind of elitism.

Mr. Prosek: They're living proof of what I think is called technocracy—the tendency of some folks to get too technical in any pursuit. Technocracy takes people away from the simplicity and beauty of fishing, and they lose sight of the original reason behind why you want to do it.

Fishing began out of necessity—people had to eat—then somehow it became a recreation, mostly with Walton, and people started to then regard it as kind of a metaphor for life.

Mr. Sloan: Walton took this sport, in his own words, as sort of a religion. We know that he was an Anglican. My personal belief is that there's a pantheism involved when I am fishing, either in a stream or the ocean. God may be in a church or temple, but he also may be found on a trout stream, and certainly I feel God is out in the ocean when I'm fishing there.

Mr. Prosek: There's no doubt that a lot of people do feel a kind of a spiritual source when they get away and escape their daily jobs. Walton was doing the same thing. He was escaping: *The Compleat Angler* proceeds with two characters, a fisherman and a hunter, walking out of the center of London to fish the River Lee, which is a tributary of the Thames. Metaphorically, though, when they walk out of London, they're not only escaping their daily jobs to go fishing but they're leaving behind the Cromwellian suppression that was taking place in London and all the strife inherent in a civil war. And I do Walton regarded fishing as somewhat of a religion. Well, on Sunday mornings he probably went to church, but shortly after that he got his fishing rod and headed down to the stream.

Mr. Sloan: What kind of tackle Walton would have used on these streams?

Mr. Prosek: He describes using a wooden rod, probably an eighteen-footer, that may have been made of greenheart, and then a length of line, about the same length as the rod, made of braided horsehair, which tapered down to sometimes just one single hair. But they didn't really cast the fly. They just sort of reached out and dapped it on the surface. They liked a little breeze that would help them blow the fly across the stream, if the breeze was blowing in the right direction. It was kind of simple, but I'm sure it was very effective.

Mr. Sloan: What were flies like in those days?

Mr. Prosek: They probably looked like some of our contemporary wet flies. They didn't have the various stiff-hackle dry flies that people like Theodore Gordon and Edward R. Hewitt made famous here in the United States. I'd think they were just some feathers and thread tied on a hook. They didn't have fly-tying vices back then; they just made the flies while holding them between their fingers.

I myself used to tie some little ant flies from single hairs from a golden-colored mane of a horse named Rheingold that lived down the street from me when I was a kid. I had an opportunity to use these Rheingold flies on some difficult trout in England. I caught a nice trout on one of them, which was sort of a nice continuum, since I was catching a fish with the same material Walton used for his line and maybe some of his flies. It just sort of extended the whole experience for me.

Mr. Sloan: What about access to streams in England? You stated that some of the streams were owned by the same families for centuries. Was it difficult getting on the water Walton himself fished?

Mr. Prosek: It's good that they've been private for centuries because they're still in very good condition. As far as access is concerned, some streams, like the River Dove, have public footpaths. As far as getting permission to fish on any one of Walton's rivers, you can buy some good day tickets for maybe twenty pounds. So for thirty dollars a day, you can fish a really good stretch of water. Otherwise, you have to figure out how to meet some people, unless you're going to pay a hundred pounds a day to fish a beat on the River Test. I did something as simple as calling the Izaak Walton Museum in Great Bridgeford near Stafford, where Walton was born, asking if anybody could take me fishing on the River Dove. But in other cases I made some friends through Yale alumni over in England. Friends of friends of theirs owned fishing rights to some of the better rivers. I built a network of people who fished and became friends with some members of the Fly Fishers' Club in London.

Mr. Sloan: Another thing that was interesting to me was the discussion in your book about otters. I know how destructive they can be, eating trout like popcorn. The funny thing that struck me was that Walton had the same problem with otters four hundred years ago.

Mr. Prosek: In fact, that's how Walton meets the hunter in the opening chapter of *The Compleat Angler.* Remember, the hunter is walking out of London with the fisherman. The hunter is going to hunt otters, and so they get along because otters kill the fish so the fisherman likes the otter hunter.

Mr. Sloan: And what was Walton's comment about grayling in the book? Did he consider them a trash fish?

Mr. Prosek: No, Walton did not consider grayling a trash fish, but in some streams now they do. In the Itchen as well as the

Test, the river-keepers were telling me to keep and kill the grayling as well as the rainbow trout in some cases because apparently there were never any grayling native to the River Itchen, and they just wanted the native brown trout in there. But the brown trout they have in there now are from all over different parts of England and even Europe. They're not necessarily the original native strain of brown trout.

Mr. Sloan: Do we make too much of a fish's native strain? As long as the trout are happy and in a suitable environment and feeding well, shouldn't we be satisfied?

Mr. Prosek: In some streams, maybe. But where you know that the original fish are already gone, it doesn't really matter. If you have a stream that has native, indigenous fish in it, you don't want to be putting in a non-native fish. There are places, like in Turkey, for instance, where there are many beautiful native brown trout streams that have not been contaminated at all because they haven't introduced non-native trout to them.

Mr. Sloan: How far east in Turkey do you have to go before you've got some trout fishing?

Mr. Prosek: I traveled with a friend of mine from Southern Austria throughout Turkey, and we caught trout in the northwest and in the southwest right near the Mediterranean coast. So, you don't have to go far from Istanbul. We also caught trout in the headwaters of the Euphrates in Eastern Turkey, and we fished in the headwaters of the Tigris near the Iraqi border, where the Kurds are fighting the Turkish Army. In short, there are trout all over the place.

Mr. Sloan: And they're doing well?

Mr. Prosek: As well as can be expected. They're doing well despite places where people fish for them with nets and, even worse, explosives.

Mr. Sloan: James, before we wrap up here, I think we ought to mention your Web site, www.troutsite.com. What's on your site?

Mr. Prosek: The site's got information about the book and reprints of some articles I've written. You'll also find information on fishing in different places around the country.

Mr. Sloan: James, it's been good talking to you. I want to thank you again for taking us back in history to Izaak Walton with your new book, *The Complete Angler: A Connecticut Yankee Follows in the Footsteps of Walton*, published by Harper and Collins. You'll go trout fishing again soon, I'm sure. Meanwhile, good luck with the book and your other travels.

Stephen Sloan is the author of the recently published Fly Fishing Spoken Here *by Meadow Run Press, a collection of interviews from his popular radio show* The Fishing Zone *. Mr. Sloan also manages to get out on the water once in a while as evidenced by his 44 world records IGFA.*

Snowstorm, Beaverkill
Galen Mercer
Oil on Canvas
1987

Winter Kill

Thomas Robert Barnes

It will rain soon.
Brusque as calm fed up is bored with itself
weather breaks by fallen full cups
and we are left to pick through
its shatterings, seepage skittered to gloom.

Just before it and mostly after,
it's the silence we keep
that all of nature pause to inflect
for long after faltering light
its clapped parentheses still ring like an echo

of how we stopped to watch
last reflection of peak upon the lake,
glimmer in two overfilled hands of water ,
barbed nicks of quartz and feldspar,

and in its diorama flickered candle upon mantle.
Where we carved a place to stand upon the ledge
is where we cached the fish we'd caught in snow
enough to sup before we slept

for taking golden trout from this high up
seems kin to stealing coin from the offering cup
and the best we can manage is gratefulness
and be careful not to slip,

slink under the nose
where light fell like a closing door ,
its dull blade sharp enough to lop the mountain like a loaf,
flesh of open bread still warm upon the rock,
glowing stamp still warm upon our mind.

And just before we descend, hop scree,
fall in waiting arms deeper shadow of the trees,
scarlet furred manzanita blurry as running mice
and pure as white blood trickled,
car lamps wending the valley far below.

Bloodknot

Standing beside church pool it snows to beat the band.
You twist the monofilament back over itself.
Since you are right handed you hold the place
where the lines bend to meet with your left
and begin again the other side
until you've crossed the ends to make the knot.

You've stopped to show me before
in Yellowstone and Tahoe.
You were younger then and
more impatient like our father,
the pressure to learn quickly
unfortunately inverse of the desired effect.

Now forty years later
my eyes are not what they used to be
and I wish for the glasses I forgot to bring
to watch you dab saliva on the string
to lubricate these contorting bodies
as you pull the ends to make them writhe.

It is out of caring, yours, that I believe
I make the effort to want to see
this time how the knot is made.
And even when you'd held the creamy brown trout
up to show me before you let it go
all I could think of was the snow flake you'd pointed out
that stopped to perch where the leaders came together,
the bloodknot touched by a watchful father.

Scales

Even before the hit
I almost asked,
what color is it of blue?

Under water
a shadow smiles its lack of concern
as it is being eaten by light.

I look past the pliers
that knocked him cold
and the bottom of the boat

freckled with the splatter of his blood.
How could water not miss him,
the company of him

passing through its fingers?
His blue skin shivers
less and less.

This is how a bell
sings to its echo,
a shimmy of dwindled parentheses

and how he gently swims past
what his body
is beginning to forget.

Angling The Meadow

I too hurry
hungry to be home
but await soft breathing
bells of chickadees
slightly above ski crunched snow.

Stippled air of their tiny notes
succincts a map of failing light
that if I'd come a different way
down the mountain tonight
might have missed their plucking.

The rule of light is never broken
but I keep adding corollaries of perspective.
shadows umber blue
as acorn masa
palely echo slapped metate.

Turn just once
to see it blush,
my crooked path
tugged like string across
aspenned fingers.

Kiss

The sleet that came
To itch the glass

It or me who changed my dream

And led me to your neck

The smile that helped me in
The tucked chin

A moan softer than stripped wind

The welcome rise of trout
To kiss

The underside of waters skin

Thomas Robert Barnes is a screenwriter and backcountry skier by trade. His writing tends to follow his interests in sports and history but like any good dog it has a mind of its own. His work has appeared in many small magazines, mostly in New York.

Fish Market
Carl Armin Hansen
Etching
1928

Hunting the Hunt

James Rudaitis

*W**e who go a-fishing are a peculiar people. Like other men and women in many respects, we are like one another, and like no others, in other respects.*

—W. C. Prime, I Go A-Fishing *(1873)*

The first fly rod I every cast was a split cane belonging to my father. It was a Granger, a pretty honey-colored rod with light green wraps. My father and I stood in our backyard where under his patient tutelage I struggled to mimic the long graceful loops I had watched him extend so effortlessly so many times, he standing in a stream and I sitting on the bank guarding our lunch. When I turned twelve, he bought me a cane rod of my own, a little 7-foot Horrocks-Ibbotson. When fiberglass rods came along, I had to have one; earnings from my paper route financed a 7-1/2 foot Heddon. Both rods served me well right through high school. Then came the navy, then college; during those years fishing was put on the back burner so long I scarcely remembered what the rods looked like.

After college I inventoried my meager tackle. The 7-1/2 foot glass rod was gone, having succumbed to a car door. The little 7-foot H-I showed its scars from the small bushy streams I had fished as a kid—one guide missing, another about to come off. Also, the tip section had developed such a nasty set that when I tried it out, I was able to master a curve cast without even trying. My father's Granger was now in my possession, left to me when he passed away. It still looked good, but together with its age and a lot of use, casting it gave new meaning to the term "parabolic-action."

Obviously I needed to do some shopping.

Leo's Sporting Goods catered mostly to spin-fishermen. He had a few discount store glass rods with guides a mile apart and for fly reels a couple of cheap make-believe Hardys. I had to resort to mail order. Soon after I ordered a few items, I became inundated with fishing catalogs, some outfits sending multiple copies just in case I misplaced the first one they had sent. Before long I was on a first name basis with the UPS man.

I still had not gotten a rod. The catalogs made it clear that fiberglass rods were a thing of the past; cane rods, though scarce, were available but carried hefty prices. Graphite was king; catalogs touted its merits with overflowing acclaim. I was hesitant, but I didn't want the season to end before I made up my mind. I ordered an 8-1/2 foot, 6-weight graphite.

The new rod performed well; it had a crisp no-nonsense feel to it and could slap out line into a stiff breeze with gusto. I was pleased but not entirely. It was a brute of a casting machine, but somehow it lacked the grace of the slower, gentler rods I grew up with. Maybe graphite just wasn't for me.

Toward the end of the season when I thought the floodgates had closed on the deluge of fishing catalogs I'd been receiving, another one came. It was a classy one almost rivaling the Orvis catalog. It was from the H. L. Leonard Rod Co. Leonard saved the best for last as the entire last page was devoted to one model, the Leonard Hunt. The rods shown on previous pages, while quite nifty, paled in comparison. The Hunt had a rich chestnut hue, the silk windings a delicate rose tipped in brown. Its 8-foot length was ideal. The three-piece model would be nicely suited to the peanut-shell trunk of my Volkswagen. This was my dream rod, but the price was scary. With rent, car payments, and a student loan, my checkbook was usually on the disabled list for most of each month. Then there was a diamond ring coming up—Gwen had agreed to marry me.

* * *

The week before Christmas I took a few days off to visit my mother in Pennsylvania. On a cold but sunny morning I got on the Thruway to head south to Newburgh where I'd take I-84 to Scranton. There would be one stop along the way—Central Valley, home of Leonard Rod.

Walking into the Leonard Store I had the feeling I imagined a first-time father might have waiting to see his newborn. "I'd like to see a Leonard Hunt, a three-piece one if you have any in stock."

"Sure, but you can't cast it. This one's being shipped out today."

The clerk produced a brown saddle-leather rod tube, withdrew the rod sections ever so carefully, gently laying them on the counter. "It takes a five line," he said, "which is a good all-rounder for trout. To me a six is a clothesline and a four is like sewing thread." As I picked up the butt section, I felt I couldn't swallow my own saliva. The reel fittings and ferrules were a dark bluish pewter color—no shiny tinsel on this baby to spook trout. The shrink-wrapped cork grip was flawless.

"Do you want to see where it's going?" the clerk asked as he placed a sturdy cardboard mailing tube on the counter and rolled it forward so the mailing label faced me.

As I knew the rod was not being shipped to me, I didn't much care where it was going, but I indulged him. "Sure…yeah." My eyes caught the bottom line of the address then moved upwards. WASHINGTON, D.C…. PENNSYLVANIA AVENUE…MRS. ROSELYN CARTER.

"Wow! It's going to the White House?"

"Yep, a little Christmas present for the president from his wife."

"Does the leather rod case come with it?" I asked.

"Nope, that's seventy-five bucks extra. She didn't order one with the rod, but we threw one in gratis since it's for the President."

I thanked him and left knowing there'd probably be a lot of deep-pocketed guys ordering a Hunt that spring, but it was doubtful I'd be one of them.

Back on the Thruway the odometer counted off miles

until the I-84 exit finally appeared. Economy always being the story of my life, my car had no radio. With no music and just the monotonous lawn mower drone of a Volkswagen engine, I was left to carry on a conversation with myself.

I imagined what a blast it would be to buy the Hunt and go fishing with my so-called friend Jimmy Crandall. Jimmy always liked and always had "the good stuff"; he'd do a double take when he saw the rod. His family was well off; his father had owned a Mercedes-Benz dealership. After his father retired Jimmy took over the dealership. Undaunted by not having made it through Cornell, Jimmy was determined to make it in the business world. Another showroom was built, and he was also selling Cadillacs. Then came a marina business on Long Island Sound. Jimmy did O.K.

I knew Jimmy since the first grade. We both liked to fish, and we palled around together all through school except for ninth grade when his father shipped him off to a military school in Virginia where Jimbo established a school record for the most demerits earned by a student in a single semester. He was the prince of one-upmanship. He still has the charming habit of waving a tongue-moistened finger through the air and snickering: "Score one for me." Jimmy's feats were often enhanced by his stories, which often nudged the borders of reality. More than once after he'd left our house I remember my father saying, "If bullshit were music, that kid would be a brass band."

He wasn't a half-bad guy, though. I remember lying in a naval hospital bed wondering if I was going to croak from an infection whose cure baffled the doctors when in walked Jimmy, and my mother and father. They had flown down to Pensacola to see me—Jimmy paid for their flight.

A large green highway sign loomed ahead, its white letters alerting me that Scranton was 18 miles ahead. I got my mind off Jimmy and back on the Hunt. I was definitely going to get one, but not now—in a year, maybe two. Leonard Rod had been in business for a long time and they'd be around for years to come.

* * *

In late March I drove to Leo's to pick up a fishing license, the one item tackle catalogs did not carry. Leo had moved to a new shop in the mall on Fox Road. In his new place I was glad to see a lot more fly tackle—fly reels outnumbered spinning reels and metal lures took a back seat to trays of trout flies. One of the rod racks at the rear of the store held only fly rods. Next to the Fenwicks were some cane rods—Leonard's. First in line was a two-piece Hunt. I glanced at the price tag.

"Leo, this rod's fifty bucks more than in the catalog."

"You mean last year's catalog. They all went up. The three-piecers went up a hundred," Leo informed me. "I have some nice Duracanes for less if you're interested."

Maybe waiting a year wasn't such a good idea. Inflation has a nasty way of penalizing those who delay purchases. But the wedding was two months away. I'd have to wait.

Spring and summer passed quickly the year I got married. Not much time for fishing, too busy moving to a bigger apartment, buying furniture, and just getting acclimated to married life. Before I knew it the kitchen calendar showed November and the Friday after Thanksgiving, I sat nearly dozing, having overdosed on leftover turkey. There was a large ad in the evening paper's sports section: Leo's Sporting Goods— Going Out Of Business Sale—Everything 50% Off. I raced to the phone hoping Leo would still be open. He was and he still had the Leonard Hunt, and yes it was 50% off.

I planned on getting to Leo's shop early Saturday morning, but thanks to Johnny Carson we slept late and I didn't get there until almost eleven. The place was crowded. I wedged my way through the bargain hunters to the back wall where the fly rods were. The Hunt was not there. I inched my way back to the front of the store where Leo was.

"Where's the Leonard Hunt rod, Leo? Did you put it away for me?"

"No, you didn't tell me to. That Crandall guy who owns the car place down the road was in here an hour ago and he bought it."

"Son of a bitch!" I half shouted, half whispered clenching my fists. Score one for Jimmy.

* * *

Two years passed and we said goodbye to the '70s. Gradually affluence was becoming less of a stranger to us. I finally passed the CPA exam and got a hefty raise. Gwen, who had been working at the community college library, was promoted to director. We made a down payment on a house and traded the Volkswagen for a new Ford station wagon. Life was good; I could now afford a Hunt.

My long awaited day came on a Saturday morning in January. With credit card in hand I dialed Leonard Rod only to learn their phone was disconnected. I called information, but they were of no help. What happened to Leonard Rod? I called Leo to see if he might know. Leonard Rod was now defunct—out of business! According to Leo they had been going downhill every since Johnson's Wax took over the company; operations ceased with a bankruptcy sale a few months ago.

I refused to give up—the chase was on. That winter I wrote to several used rod dealers, but listings for a Hunt were rare. A dealer in Connecticut had one listed in fair condition at a very reasonable price. Hoping for the best I made the long drive there, but the rod's condition might better be described as pitiful. One tip top was broken off, a lot of hook digs, a chunk of cork missing from the grimy cork grip, the butt cap dented, and a nasty dinger in the rod tube.

Hope dwindled until one day I received a flyer from the Thomas & Thomas Company and saw listed:

LEONARD HUNT 8ft. #5
3 pc., 2 tips
Orig. sack & tube. Mint. $1,050.

I was on the phone in a flash. The rod was still available and they'd put it aside for me tomorrow, but just for that one-day.

I took the next day off and drove to Turners Falls, getting there around noon. A big burly guy at the shop told me the rod was no longer available. He had called my house that morning to tell me but I had already left. What hadhappened was that a woman who was going through a divorce had brought the rod in to be sold on consignment a couple of weeks ago. But early that morning the husband appeared along with his lawyer claiming that the rod belonged to him, and his soon-to-be ex-wife had no right to sell it. I drove home disgusted.

April came and went and I was still Huntless. In early May I got a call from Jimmy Crandall. Mercedes-Benz was having some sort of pow-wow for some of its northeast dealers and their wives. It was being held at the Beaverkill Valley Inn in the Catskills. Would I be interested in going? Wouldn't cost me a dime, he'd even drive, and we could fish. He guaranteed the Hendricksons would be popping up in droves this time of year, and besides the inn was located on the upper Beaverkill, on a stretch so private even God couldn't fish there.

"O.K., don't make it sound too good, Jimmy. I'll go."

Thursday night a little before six Jimmy showed up in a new 450-SEL and we were on our way.

"The winters really hang on up here," he commented. "Three weeks ago I was down in Pennsylvania fishing; not a lick of snow and the trees were already greening up."

"Where'd you go in Pennsylvania?"

"Spruce Creek. It's about twenty miles outside of State College, where Penn State is."

"How was the fishing? Any good?"

"Pretty good. Lot of trout, but they weren't pushovers. I only got eight that weekend. I'd like to go back in early June when there's supposed to be some good Green Drake hatches."

"How'd you hear about it?"

"An old friend of my father's who's a bigwig in the state's Democratic Party down there has a place near the stream; he invited me down. We fished a private stretch of club water. I met Jimmy Carter while I was there," he nonchalantly added, "and I fished with him one afternoon."

"Jimmy Carter—the President?"

"Uh, huh. He fly fishes you know and so does his

wife."

"Yeah, seems to me I heard that."

We arrived on the heels of nightfall. I was anxious to
see the stream, but I could barely make it out in the dwindling
light. I could hear it though, across the meadow from the inn,
only about a nine-iron shot away. The inn was a big white clap-
board place with a wide wraparound porch. Our room opened
onto the porch.

A lot of Benz dealers and their wives were already at
the bar. Cocktail hour was well underway and the lounge
buzzed with small talk. It was obvious these imbibers were
devotees of the good life. I felt out of place. I expected them to
be standoffish and I dreaded tiptoeing through a society minefield on my way to the bar. But I was wrong; they turned out to
be a nice bunch of people.

Dinner was buffet style and very elaborate. Later I mentioned to Jimmy that I counted eight different desserts.
"Really?" He laughed and poked my belly. "Which one did you
like best?"

Everything was going fine until we got back to the
room. Jimmy plopped in a chair and took off his shoes. The
smell of his feet would make an onion cry. I opened the window.

"It's kind of cool in here. You really want that window
open?" he asked.

"Well...uh...we could hear the sound of the stream.
That would be a nice way to fall asleep."

"Yeah, you're right. That would be nice."

Unfortunately for me, with the help of two after-dinner
cognacs Jimmy fell asleep before I did. His snoring outdid the
sound of a chain saw badly in need of a tune-up.

The next morning was dismal and overcast; a light rain
was falling. After breakfast I'd fish alone as Jimmy would be
tied up at a meeting.

"What are you going to use this morning?" he asked.

"I'll probably drag the bottom with some nymphs."

He laid his meeting-bound folders on the bed, went to
the closet and returned with a fly box.

"Here, try these," he said laying some nymphs in the palm of my hand.

Three Pheasant Tails, but unlike any nymph I'd seen before. Each had a gold metal bead between the thorax and the hook eye. "Did you tie these?" I asked.

"No. I picked them up last summer when I was in Germany. They're killers. Try 'em."

Had he fished with the German Chancellor? I didn't ask.

While not overflowing its banks, the water was high—wadding staff high. I spent two hours working my way downstream, first with my old standby Hare's Ear, then with a Zug Bug, but no luck. After a break for some thermos coffee I worked back upstream with a Tellico nymph, but still no takers. Just below the bridge I managed to hook two nice browns on—you guessed it—one of Jimmy's gold BB nymphs.

The morning drizzle stopped and spears of sunlight sliced through a steel wool sky. On the porch I placed my rod on two protruding wall pegs and hung up my waders. The door to our room swung open.

"I thought I heard you out here. I hope you had a better morning than I did; I was so bored I got a headache. How'd you do? Catch anything?"

"Two."

"Is that all? Let's go eat," he said.

After lunch I stood on the porch waiting for Jimmy to get rigged up. He looked like a leprechaun, his waders made from that new wet suit material and contouring his spindly legs and potbelly. He opened a leather rod case and out came a 3-piece Leonard Hunt.

"Jimbo, that's not the Leonard you beat me to a while back at Leo's is it? The one he had was a 2-piecer wasn't it?"

"Yeah, I gave that one to my father for Father's Day."

"Where'd you get this one?"

"I, uh…picked it up the weekend I was in Pennsylvania…a little tackle shop near State College. The guy had some used rods and I spied this one. It's practically new, I got a good deal on it."

The afternoon was a bust even though the sun was shining. More black flies than Henricksons appeared. Rises were few, but we persisted in foolishly flogging the surface with dries but with little success. Jimmy caught one small brown, I caught nothing. A little before five, it clouded over and the sky opened up, rain coming down with a vengeance. We double-timed it back to the inn.

With the grace of an one-legged ballerina, Jimmy struggled out of his waders. "These neoprenes are nice, but they're a pain in the ass to get on and off. Now as my father used to say, 'Let's get out of these wet clothes and into a dry martini.'"

Saturday was a clone of Friday—off and on rain. We went fishless. Saturday night a long steady soaker settled in, and on Sunday morning we said so long to a high, rain-swollen stream.

* * *

One night in early September I got a call from Jimmy. He was selling his Hunt rod, a steal at six hundred dollars; was I interested? No check though, he wanted cash. He'd be over tomorrow night around seven. The next night he was standing in my den laying the rod sections on my tying table. The rod was in excellent shape, no hook digs, no sets. He seemed nervous and in a hurry.

"I had my name sanded off on the butt section...then revarnished," he spurted. "You can get a rod maker to put yours on it if you like."

He took his money and left, declining an offer from my wife to stay for some cake and coffee. I walked him to his car; a big Jeep lookalike with the words "Range Rover" tattooed above the grill. I don't drive an expensive car, and no I don't require plane tickets to get to the places I fish. But I now owned a <u>Leonard Hunt</u>! Score one for me.

When he drove away that evening I had no idea I'd probably never see him again, as two days later Jimmy made the six o'clock news and the following day's newspaper: "<u>JAMES CRANDALL, PROMINENT LOCAL...WHERE-</u>

ABOUTS UNKNOWN." It seems Jimmy had flown the coop leaving a lot of creditors hanging for close to a million dollars. The State Tax Department had closed his operation—over $80,000 sales tax unpaid. The IRS was concerned about a failed court appearance, and his Connecticut marina was belly-up in bankruptcy.

Jimmy's car business lay dormant for over a year until a Honda dealer moved into one side. Around the time a Pizza Hut opened in the adjacent former Cadillac showroom I found myself sitting in a barbershop waiting my turn. I thumbed through a back issue of an outdoor magazine in which on two adjoining pages were some small news items. A short piece about former President Jimmy Carter caught my eye. After Carter moved out of the White House and back to Georgia, he discovered that his valuable Leonard fly rod, which had been a gift from his wife, had been stolen. Carter regarded the loss of the rod as worse than the loss of the election. I didn't believe it! That probably was the same rod I held at the Leonard Shop some years back. As soon as I got back home I went directly to my tackle closet to make sure my Hunt was still there.

* * *

Years had slipped by me pretty fast; I'd turn 40 next month. My son Robert now has a little sister, Rachel. The day Robert was born I ordered him a 7-1/2 foot Winston for his future use. I only fished it once. Honest. But so far he has shown little enthusiasm for learning how to fly cast. My wife says to be patient, wait a while.

"How long should I wait? The kid's already eight years old!" I said aloud but to no one. I was alone in the house, Gwen gone to Syracuse for a librarian's conference, the kids at her mother's. The house was quiet, the TV, dishwasher, and clothes dryer, all mute. Maybe even a house requires some noiseless downtime occasionally.

I sat in my den trying to decide what to do with the rest of a kickback Friday night. I had enough leaders tied up to last two seasons; my fly boxes were organized and reorganized. I decided to read. Two unread books lay on my table, a small paperback on nymphing, and a book of outdoor recollections by Jimmy Carter. I settled in with the Jimmy Carter book, <u>An Outdoor Journal</u>.

Some pages later I put the book down with a shudder. I had gotten to the part where Carter was recalling some of his weekend fishing trips to Pennsylvania while he was still in the White House. The stream? Spruce Creek—the same stream Jimmy Crandall mentioned when he told me he had fished with the President. Maybe it wasn't a baloney story. That magazine article…President Carter's rod stolen…the rod I bought from Jimmy just like the one I saw at the Leonard shop before it was shipped off to the White House.

"<u>Son of a bitch</u>!" Did Jimmy steal the President's rod and then sell it to me?

I went to the closet and got it out. I laid the butt section under the magnifying lamp on my tying table and scrutinized the area that had been sanded and revarnished. Just above the hookkeeper I could barely make out what looked to be the lower loop of a handwritten, "J", surely part of the first letter of the name Jimmy—but which Jimmy? I toyed with the idea of taking it to an FBI lab to see if they could determine whose name had been written on it. But that seemed doubtful as except for the faint little loop, the rest had been sanded off thoroughly. I put the rod away.

I'll probably never know whom it belonged to originally. If it were the President's, it should eventually be retired to a fly fishing museum and not end up in the closet of some ham-and-egger like me. All I know is that my search for a Hunt was over, and I am glad. President Carter's was probably still going on. I felt sorry for him.

James Rudaitis is a graduate of Wyoming Seminary Preparatory School and has earned degrees at the Indiana Institute of Technology and Union College. A retired mathematics professor, he now lives with his wife Susan in upstate New York—midway between the trout streams of the Adirondacks and those of the Catskills. He is a long-time devotee of the fly rod and is hopelessly addicted to old fishing books. His writings have appeared in Fly Fisherman *and* Sporting Tales. *Currently he is at work on a collection of fly fishing short stories.*

Theodore Gordon
Photograph
Courtesy of American Museum of Fly Fishing
1915

Theodore Gordon

Austin McK. Francis

In an accident of history, both the modern dry fly and the brown trout were brought to America at the same time, creating a double revolution. Trying to catch a brown trout with a dry fly on the rivers of the Catskills was the beginning of the art of dry-fly fishing as we know it in this country. Theodore Gordon—with his pioneering experiments, discoveries, and reporting—was the key figure in bringing about this new era.

Gordon was born of a well-to-do family in Pittsburgh in 1854. Fly fishing from the age of fourteen, he lived a remarkable life, almost nonexistent in our day. A man of taste and intelligence, a restrained yet warm and exciting fishing writer, Gordon fled civilization for a retreat on the Neversink River. He put one thing only into his mind—the stream—and sustained it there unflaggingly for a great many years. An inexplicable performance, probably never to be duplicated.

Gordon's rare dedication to the Sport came about by virtue of an illness that barred him from the life of a stockbroker or other conventional calling and kept him in the mountains. That at any rate was his excuse for giving his good mind exclusively for many years to the subject of fly fishing. He spit blood during his last three years and died, May 1, 1915, of tuberculosis. What we really know of him is that he lived a sweet, good life, perhaps the only man ever to express with his whole life the ideal of the anglers' brotherhood.

Theodore Gordon was one of the first to recognize and promote the virtues of brown trout. Looking back over the marvelous fishing he had had since his first brown in 1889, Gordon wrote in 1903:

Fifteen years ago, in many of our best New York trout streams, a one-pound native trout was a big fish. In all my experiences of waters easily accessible from New York, I took but one fish of sixteen inches. Since the introduction of the brown trout, all this is changed. The average size of trout taken has much increased, and many fish of two pounds are caught every season with fly. Not only is this the case, but not a year passes that a number of immense fish are not hooked by fly fishermen. I mean fish weighing from four to six pounds. These usually escape, owing to the light tackle used, but they afford a man a sensation that he is in no danger of forgetting to the last day of his life.

The first mention of "dry" fly fishing in America appeared in 1864 in Thad Norris's *The American Angler's Book*. Norris was fishing with a friend on Willowemoc Creek, the fish were "shy," and his friend "put on a Grannom for a stretcher, and a minute Jenny Spinner for a dropper. . . .By cracking the moisture from them between each throw, he would lay them so lightly on the glassy surface that a brace of Trout would take them at almost every cast, before they sank down or were drawn away. . . .Here was an exemplification of the advantage of keeping one's flies dry."

Theodore Gordon had prepared himself for the coming of the dry fly. He had grown up with *The American Angler's Book* (his "book of books"), and from it he had learned to face upstream and fish his wet flies dry. He had fished through the demise of the brook trout into the rise of the brown. And he was well connected with England and the rest of the angling world through his correspondence and readings. So it was natural that he should hear of Frederic M. Halford's crusade for the dry fly in England and his trend-setting books, *Floating Flies and How to Dress Them* (1886), and *Dry Fly Fishing in Theory and Practice* (1889).

Gordon devoured both of Halford's books and wrote to ask him for more information on this new phenomenon. Halford's reply is now flyfishing history; on February 22, 1890, he sent back a letter offering to help Gordon create new floating patterns specifically for American waters. Clipped to his letter, each identified alongside, were approximately fifty of his favorite dry flies. "And thus," wrote John McDonald, "The dry fly winged its way to the New World."

This event has come to symbolize the arrival of the dry fly in America partly because it involved a dramatic, documentable exchange between two angling giants, but mainly because Gordon used Halford's flies and advice to create the first American dry-fly patterns. Actually, Gordon was one of a growing number of Americans who knew of Halford and were experimenting with English dry flies and wets fished dry, beginning with Thad Norris in the early 1860s. Dry-fly articles had already appeared in American periodicals of the 1870s, and the first American books to mention dry-fly tactics and tying were published in the 1880s. What sets Gordon apart from the other early American dry-fly enthusiasts is the fact that *he scrutinized English dry flies and dry-fly tactics and found them unsuited to American trout streams.* So he started from scratch to identify native insects, design new patterns, and perfect his own presentational techniques. Where the others accepted what was available, Gordon was inquisitive, skeptical, and innovative.

When Gordon brought Halford's letter home from the post office, his hands must have trembled as he opened it and viewed the famous dry-fly master's creations—Pale Watery Dun, Little Marryat, Orange Bumble, Jenny Spinner, Welshman's Button, and all the others. "The bacilli or microbe which infects the dry fly entered my system," wrote Gordon, "and the attack which followed was quite severe." He went all-English, with imported rod, dry flies, gossamer silkworm gut, and "all other prescriptions which I presumed necessary to effect a cure," but soon discovered that the English equipment and even the dry-fly tactics were not working to his satisfaction. The insects on which Halford patterned his flies differed from ours, and the placid chalk streams of Hampshire were nothing like the tumbling, freestone streams of the Catskills.

Gordon realized that he was now confronted with both a great opportunity and a difficult challenge. Undaunted, he started with the basics, using the English theories as a general guide, and created dry-fly patterns that worked on American streams. For this he had to devise a crude system for classifying stream insects before there was ever an American stream entomology. He bemoaned the lack of such, and the fact that "an angler will often be at a loss in trying to identify an insect which he finds is attractive to the fish." But he persisted in his conviction that "a copy of the natural fly upon the water will often give one a good basket of trout when all other artificial flies are nearly, if not quite, useless."

An incident that occurred on the Beaverkill in 1906 perfectly illustrates this premise. Gordon ran into M. T. Davidson for the first time while both men were fishing. Davidson had raised an exceptionally large fish and, casting repeatedly, had been unable to hook it. He eyed Gordon's tackle, judged that he was a real fisherman, and told him where the big trout was, but Gordon would not fish for it. Instead, he gave a brilliant lesson in matching the hatch, described by Davidson a few years later in a letter to *Forest and Stream*:

Along the banks grew some willows, and in these Mr. Gordon found several fine specimens of the fly. After securing a large one, Mr, Gordon produced a box of feathers, gut and No, 12 fly hooks. In a remarkably short time he had tied a beautiful duplicate of the original and, handing it to me, insisted that I make another try at the old trout.

Nervously, Davidson tied on Gordon's imitation, cast for, hooked, played, and landed a 20 1/4-inch, three-pound, eight-ounce trout. The two fishermen went back to Trout Valley Farm, where they ate supper together and where Davidson christened the new fly "Gordon's Fancy," even though "fancy" flies were not supposed to be imitations of real insects.

Creating successful imitations of American stream insects was only half of Gordon's achievement. The other half was working out a dry-fly construction for American streams, where the flies, quoth McDonald, "are always being ducked by white caps, froth, converging currents, and all the movements of the stream." Halford could afford to use softer hackle, for he and his countrymen fished to the rise in quiet water, but Gordon sought a stiffer hackle and tied it as sparsely as the conditions would allow. In so doing, he gave birth to a unique American style of dry-fly tying, later perfected by his Catskill followers into the "Catskill style," typically a No. 12 or No. 14 hook, with a lean body of spun fur or stripped quill, a divided wing of lemon-colored wood-duck flank-feather barbules, and several turns of stiff cock's hackle, usually dun, ginger, or grizzly.

Even though Gordon respected Halford and numbers of other English and American dry-fly experts, he had little patience with the fast-growing "cult of the dry-fly purist." Sometimes he was tolerant: "A few ultra dry fly men may assume airs of superiority, but they are mostly good fellows. I have never known one of them to kill too many trout." Other times, he was not so tolerant, as when he wrote to Halford's wet-fly rival, G.E.M. Skues: "Mr. Halford is like many another. He has become an authority on dry-fly fishing and has been tempted in 'Ethics of the Dry Fly' to speak authoritatively on wet-fly fishing of which he knows nothing. How any man can be such an unmitigated ass as to 'flog' a slow clear river like Test or Itchen downstream, I cannot imagine." Halford had ignored the refinements of wet-fly fishing and characterized the wet-fly man as a "flogger" of the stream, which insulted Gordon's sensibilities.

Three months before he died, Gordon wrote to Steenrod, still fretting over the Skues-Halford rivalry:

Mr. Skues did rather a plucky thing some years ago. He worked out a system of wet fly fishing for the chalk dry fly streams, and killed many trout when the dry fly would not work. Then he published a book on "Minor Tactics of the Chalk Streams" that stirred up all the prejudice in the dry fly ranks. Mr. Halford was particularly fierce, and gave Skues (of course not mentioning him) the devil in his last book. I was very sorry as Halford had always been so fair for over 20 years, but he was growing old; for years he had fished only certain preserved lengths of the Test and Itchen. He was recognized as the great authority, and had become a bit prejudiced and dictatorial.

As John McDonald has observed, Theodore Gordon performed in this country the joint services of a Skues and a Halford. He arrived on the scene when Americans were fishing only wet flies and the English were going through a dry-fly revolution. In having brought about the juncture of these two great traditions, Gordon established himself as "the father of modern American angling."

Austin McK. Francis is a fly fishing historian and a business communications consultant. He has written or edited five books on fly fishing. He and his wife Rose live in New York City and fly fish in the Catskill mountains, where they have a home in the Beaverkill valley.

Thunder and Lightning
Peter Corbin
Oil on Canvas

Why Men Fish

Scott Starbuck

Julie opened the car door, ran shouting ###! ##! #! #####! at me, broke my custom British fly rod in half, and heaved my salmon midstream.

Then she became angry. "We're gg-gggoing home NOW!" said the short blonde wearing my oversized waders and fishing vest. "I'm cold. I'm not having fun. And my hair is wet. CAN'T YOU SEE MY HAIR IS WET?"

"Could you get me some more salmon eggs?" I asked. "I think I had a strike."

"WHERE ARE THEY?" she shrieked, frisking my body for the keys. Normally, I wouldn't have been opposed to an attractive, shy blonde like Julie pinning me to the grass and tearing off my clothes. But it was cold. And her hands were wet.

"Get off me and I'll tell you," I said, between uncontrollable fits of laughter. "They are behind the driver's seat in . . . in, a yellow box . . ."

"Good," she said. "I'm leaving you here with your fish, jerk. And I'm never going out with you again. I'm sorry I ever met you." She looked kind of cute, talking like a Marine Sergeant, with her hair matted down behind her ears like an angry muskrat's.

Behind the driver's seat, in the yellow box, Julie found the salmon eggs. From the words she screamed and the way the cows took off running, I got the hint the love in our relationship was probably strained again. "What's with her?" I wondered.

I may have smiled when fellow anglers paused to

watch her nervously cast four feet—in the wrong direction—
and hook a cow. But I did not laugh, as she claimed, when she
unexpectedly slipped and crashed into the icy river. Anyway, if
I did, there is no way she could have heard me above the thun-
dering applause.

For now, I asked her to kindly step back so I would not
hook her when I cast. She pointed at my lucky pig hat.
"'Hawg Killer'? What a joke! It should say 'Meat Head'," she
cackled, reaching in my tackle box for a large rusty filet knife. I
did not want to admit it, but I had come to another fork in the
road. It was either Julie or fishing: I could not have both.

Why, you may ask, would a man jeopardize a good
relationship to stand in a stream and hope for the big one?
Good question. One that is not easily answered dodging cow
pies while being chased with a large rusty filet knife. But given
the reflection and deep thought that comes with living alone,
one arrives at several revelations.

Primarily, men fish for the same reason they climb
mountains, ride wild mustangs, and travel into outer space.
While battling a blue marlin in the South Pacific or a monster
bluegill in grandpa's farm pond, their hearts beat faster, adrena-
line fills the veins, and the senses are keen and alert. It is participation in a sacred event in which the fish gives up its life so
the life of the human may continue.

One does not experience similar sensations stalking a
purse in the mall or visiting relatives. I'm sorry, I just don't.

Another reason men go fishing is to overcome bore-
dom, a problem which has been plaguing the gender since
ancient times. Evidence of this can be found on cave walls
where restless males drew fantastic pictures of themselves cap-
turing mammoth, deer, and largemouth bass.

"Stop writing on the walls, Bruno," an angry wife
would complain. "If you think you're going a-fishing, you can
just forget it!" Anthropologists theorize that crude numerals
below the pictures represent beginnings of the modern calendar,
but they are wrong. Men were simply keeping track of the
numbers of wives who left them.

My argument would not be complete without giving

due attention to psychological theory. In short, inconsistent rewards (fish) are more habit-forming than regular rewards (wife). The wife is, excuse the expression, in the bag; the lunker finning beneath the surface is not. So, if a man takes his girl-friend for a harmless canoe ride in the moonlight, she should be cautious. She may end up honeymooning at River's Inlet, British Columbia, alone.

The conflicts between a fisherman and his mate are unlikely to ever be resolved. The reason is that a fishermen views the world from an entirely different perspective than their non-or-seldom-fishing mates. To the former, quality of life is directly proportional to the amount of time spent outdoors. For the latter, this is an inverse relationship.

Peace is possible, however, if both parties are willing to compromise. In other words, the woman should never ask her man to sell his split bamboo pole, which crafted in China in the Fourth Century B.C., just to pay the electric bill. Nor should she, upon landing a 42-pound Chinook, make a face conveying all the enthusiasm of finding a rotten casserole in the refrigerator.

To do his part, the man should not make his woman row all of the time. Nor should he be overly critical if she chooses a lure "because it is pretty" and outfishes him. He should not threaten his wife with divorce for landscaping the neglected "Wildlife Safari" lawn—even if it does chop crawlers into itty-bitty chunks of worm paste and scare survivors to China.

When a compromise escapes and it becomes a clear choice between fishing and mate, why do the fish often come out thumbs up? In order to fully appreciate this phenomenon, one must look closely at the nature of man.

In the proverbial Garden, Adam was given everything he needed to be happy -- almost. And God said, more or less, "give you spring and fall Chinook, summer and winter steel-head, and the trouts." But man was not happy fishing in The River of Life. He had to have a woman also. So God gave Adam, Eve, along with all the fishes in The River, and he only asked that the two of them fish with flies only.

One day, Eve was munching on a mango when she very nearly bit a worm in half. "Wait. Don't throw that worm away," said a serpent in the mango tree. "Worms make good bait." You know the rest of the story.

So it remains that even today, men are natural sinners and bait fishermen—with at least half the blame going to the fairer sex. Anglers are almost never satisfied with only their mates, even if they are beautiful and endearing like Julie. And this is because we were anglers long before we were lovers, both in evolutionary terms and in our own short life spans.

As a result, when it comes to "my way or the highway," we choose the river.

When we die, we will no doubt be held accountable. One can imagine St. Peter stopping a fellow fisherman at the pearly gates: "Okay, my friend, I see you've been an awful husband, missed church to go fishing, and lied to employers every December for 35 years when steelhead were running." Then, raising an eyebrow, "But how far can you cast a fly?"

Scott Starbuck's poetry chapbook, The Eyes of Those Who Broke Free, *was recently published by Pudding House. His poems have appeared in Austrailia, Canada, England, India, Ireland, Poland, and widely in the United States. His work is forthcoming in* Black Bear Review *and* Storyboard 8 *(University of Guam). Inspired by the outdoor humorist Patrick F. McManus, the essay "Why Men Fish" is his first attempt at outdoor humor.*

Big Fish Eat Little Fish
Pieter van der Heyden
Engraving
1557

An Angler's Commentary on the Salvage Logging Rider

Richard K. Stoll

We could feel the dampness of spring lingering in the early morning hours, two, maybe three weeks after the passing of the vernal equinox. Sun filtering through massive old-growth Douglas Fir and Western Red Cedar brought out brightly colored American Goldfinches to feed on huckleberry and salal lining riverside glades. It had only been four months since winter floods had scoured rock-strewn meadows of debris. Early summer had come to the forests and streams of the Pacific Northwest.

Fallen alders criss-crossed riparian edges of the old growth forest. The air hung heavy with the characteristic dusky smell of delicate oyster mushrooms clinging to their decaying trunks. As we made our way over and around dead falls blocking the anglers trail, I strained to catch glimpses of each section of the river, its rushing torrents dominating the soundscape. I was looking for a secret forest shaded pool I had visited in past seasons, a home for summer steelhead. Had it survived the winter high water?

My companion and I moved up the bank to follow a ridge, then laterally into the heart of yet untouched Olympic rain forest. As we made out way through thick understory we talked in low voices so as not to disturb the trees. We had heard rumors that salvage loggers were scheduled to cut here.

Salvage? Salvage from the very diseases and rot that afflicts the collage of elderly trees nature had destined to provide food and nutrients to the forest floor, eventually succoring new generations of trees—and fish. Salvage for unsustainable jobs, at the expense of a new generation of lowland foresters growing trees where tree farms are most productive.

We wondered how in this day and age our own government agencies could let minority economic interests drive the political system to the detriment of our natural resources. This was our national forest on the very fringes of Olympic National Park. Access was by tax funded logging roads. Yet logging rights given to private companies cost taxpayer dearly, not to mention loss of irreplaceable natural resources? The amount the U.S. government spent to maintain national forest logging roads for private timber companies since 1994 has been on the order of 100 million dollars alone. The amount of this cost borne by those timber companies has been zero (*Common Cause*, Fall 95).

In both of us heartbreak accompanied memories of pristine runs and pools now exposed to sun and long since filled with the silty remnants of steep slope logging roads and skid paths. At the same time our hearts filled at the excitement of visiting an old friend in the forest. Like that now-obliterated hole we so fondly remembered, the steelhead pool that was our destination today would become our memory tomorrow. What would that memory bring?

We made our way out on to a high bank edge that I knew overlooked my secret pool. When we finally squeezed through the forest to open riverside I was at first surprised, then exhilarated, at a sight I did not expect to see. High winter water had filled the pool with pea-sized gravel and golf ball rocks. Two pairs of native King salmon finned in the gentle current near the tail out.

Where one pool fills, another forms. Such is the changing life of an undisturbed river. This pool was no longer a steelhead home, but a perfect nuptial bedroom for king salmon.

As for steelhead? They would rest upstream. John and I picked up our fly rods and prepared to move on. We wanted to enjoy the forest while there was still time.

Richard Stoll has been a professional environmental scientist and engineer for twenty five years. He is also a member of the International Game Fish Association (IGFA) International Committee and owns Northwest Angler, a West Sound fly fishing shop.

The Creation of the Satchem Run
Loucas Raptis
From *Poole and Rapid*
Ink on Paper
1997

Closing Day
James Rossbach

T he station wagon, loaded, was idling in the driveway under the towering hemlocks in front of the Club. On the bottom step of the veranda, buttoned up for the long trip home, stood the old man. In back of him friends—both young and no longer young—murmured their farewells. It had been a glorious weekend, the last of the season. Already the maples were beginning to turn, and one could feel in the September sunshine a hint of colder weather to come.

Yes, the weekend had been marvelous—and unusual. It was without a doubt because of the old man's presence. Once an angler of extraordinary skills, he now was crippled with arthritis and could no longer fish. Yet it had been he, the non-fisherman at a fishing club, who had been the center of attraction, the focus of the enjoyment they had all felt. Assembling from the stream at lunch or at a late cocktail hour before dinner, they had gathered around this former editor, as acolytes around a high priest, to share with him their triumphs and defeats of the day, to revel in his colorful recollections of streams of another era, and to cherish the barbs of his sharp wit. His wife, some years younger than he, had fished successfully, and one sensed that he identified with her tales of trout risen, hooked and landed or lost.

Now, in the late September setting sun, the whole bittersweet experience seemed to come together : the old man on the bottom step of a club he probably would never revisit, the season drawing to an end, the friendships of summer interrupted until another year. The old man seemed to sense this as he gazed out toward the stream through cataract-clouded eyes. His wife took him gently by the hand. "Come on, Doc," she said, "It's time to go."

"You're right, Mother," he answered. "You're right, as usual. Take me home."

James Rossbach was born in NYC and lived there most of his life. His angling experiences spanned some 60 years starting on a small ponds in White Plains, the Adirondacks, and northern Maine. Later trout and salmon fishing trips took him to Alaska and much of the Western and Northwestern United States, as well as Canada, Europe, Iceland, New Zealand and South America. The only prolonged interruptions were five years of active duty during World War II. Mr. Rossbach worked in the investment business for almost 35 years and was a general and, later, a limited partner of Ingalls & Snyder since 1959. He served on the boards of the Museum of the City of New York, Goodwill Industries, and the Miramichi Salmon Association. He also found time to edit The Anglers' Club Bulletin. *He was married to a patient lady who did not fish and had two married children, one of whom ties beautiful flies.*

Artist Loucas Raptis is a natural history illustrator and dedicatied fly fisherman from British Columbia.